I spy in the sky...

EDWARD GIBBS

B || F || & || F

BRUBAKER, FORD & FRIENDS

AN IMPRINT OF THE TEMPLAR COMPANY LIMITED

I spy with my little eye...

something with **purple** feathers and **small** wings.

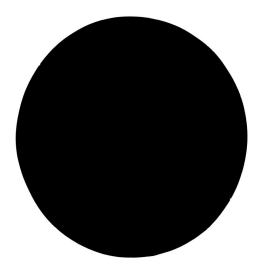

I like to feed on flowers.

I am a **hummingbird.**

I spy with my little eye...

something with **black** feathers
and **big** wings.

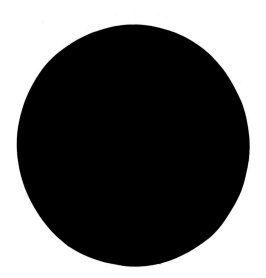

I have
a bald
head.

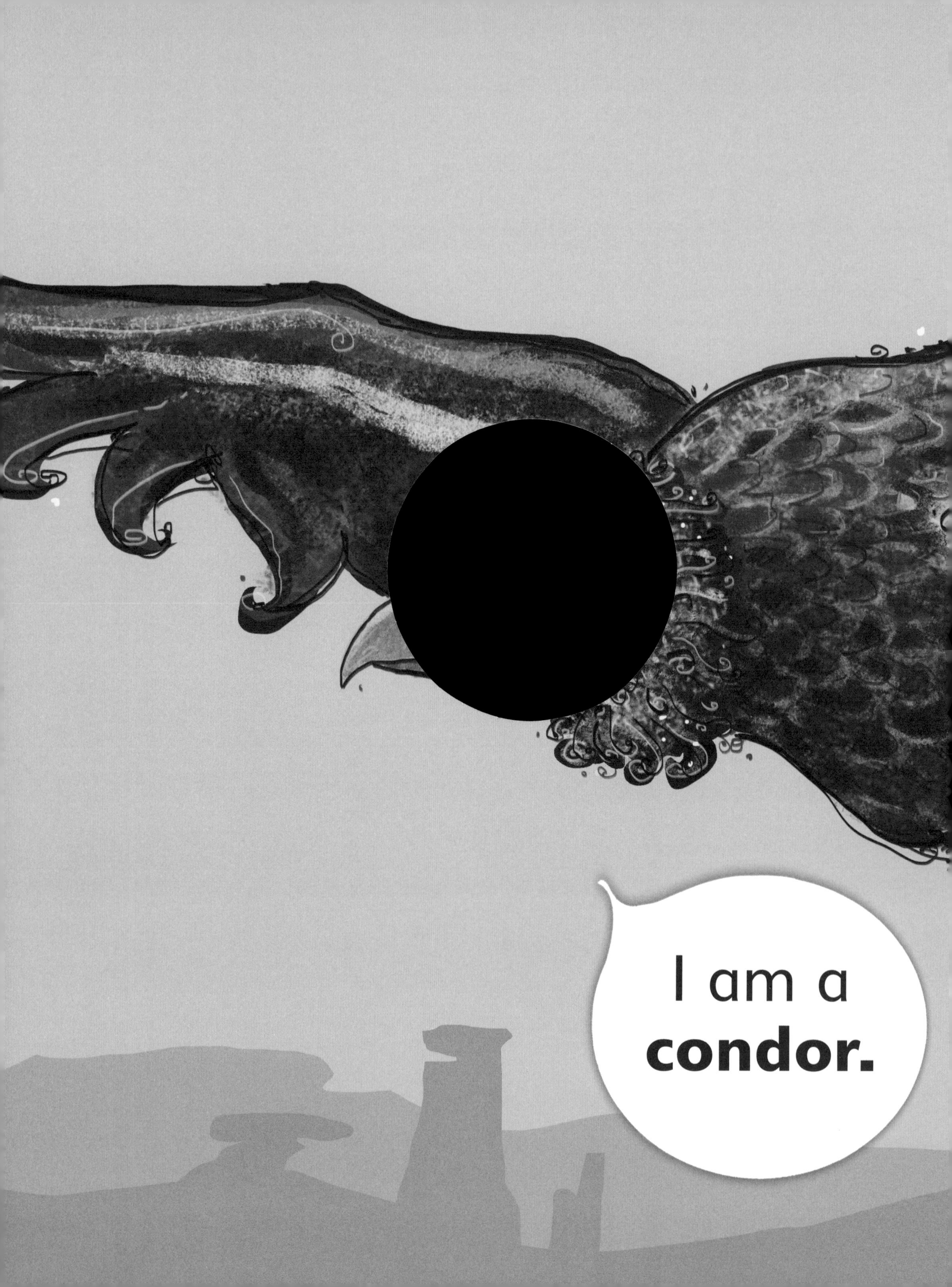
I am a **condor.**

I spy with my little eye...

something with **blue** feathers
and a **short** bill.

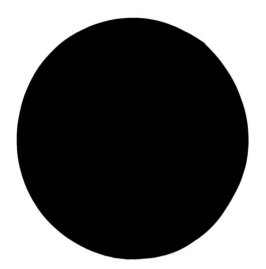

Polly
wants a
cracker.

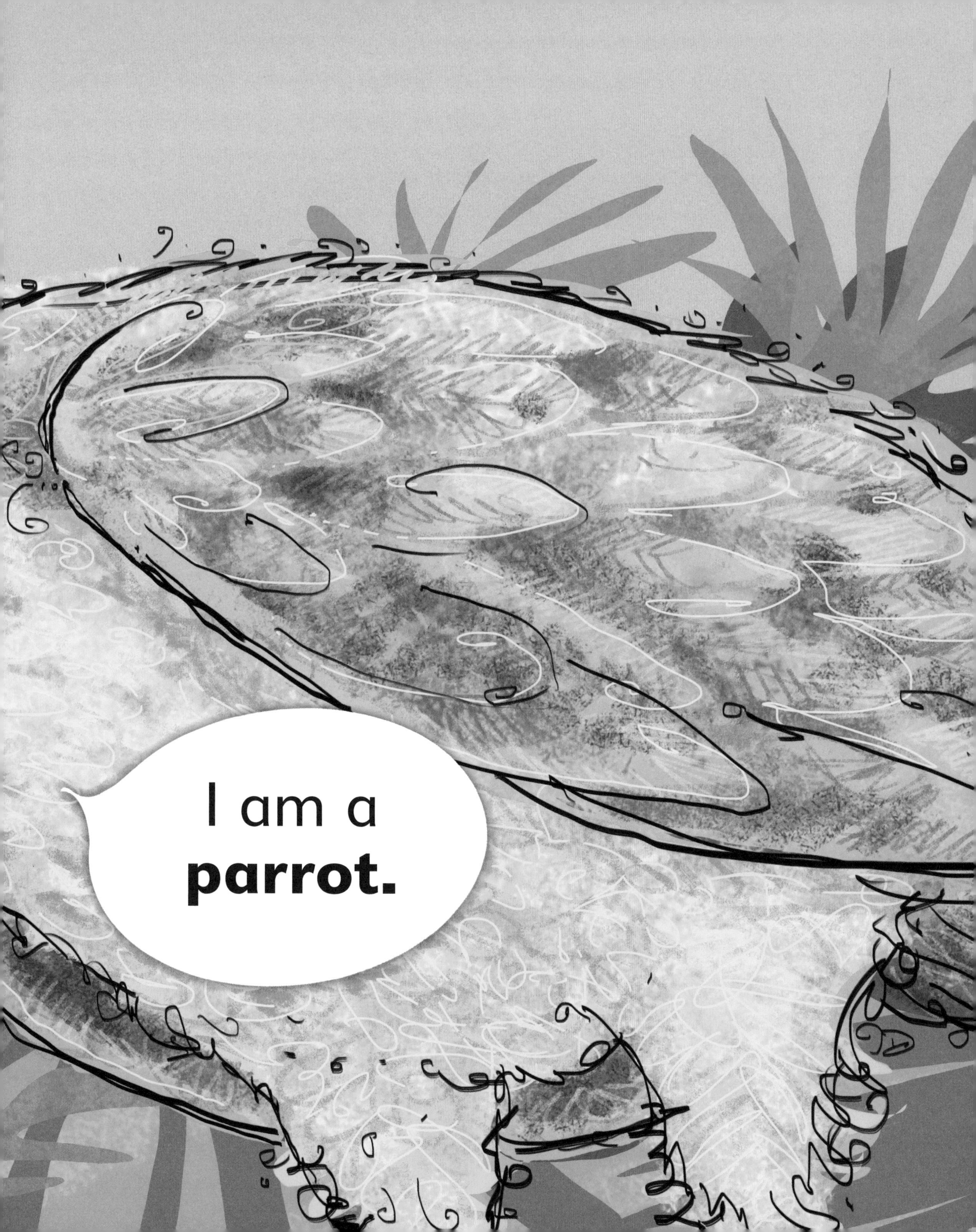
I am a **parrot.**

I spy with my little eye...

something with **white** feathers
and a **long** bill.

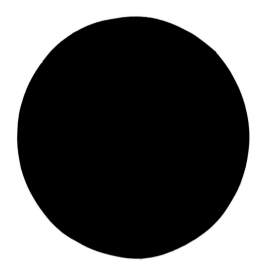

I like to
fish for
food.

I am a
pelican.

I spy with my little eye…

something with **brown** feathers
that flies very **high**.

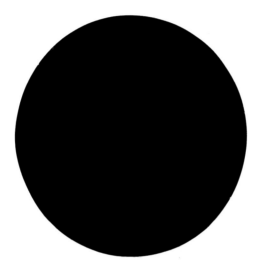

I have
sharp talons.

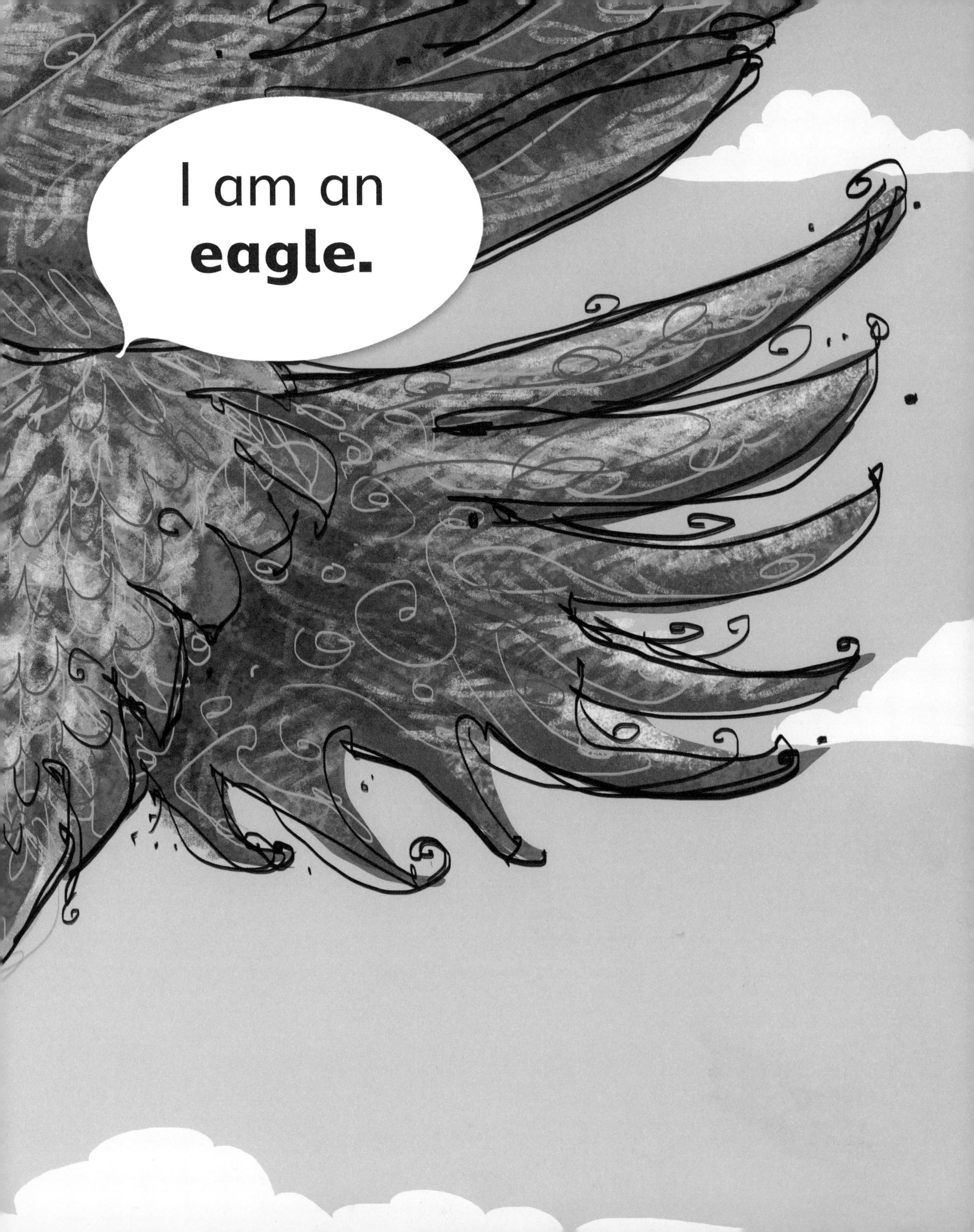
I am an **eagle.**

I spy with my little eye...

something with **multi-coloured** feathers that flies very **low**.

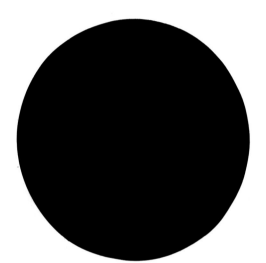

I have a spectacular tail.

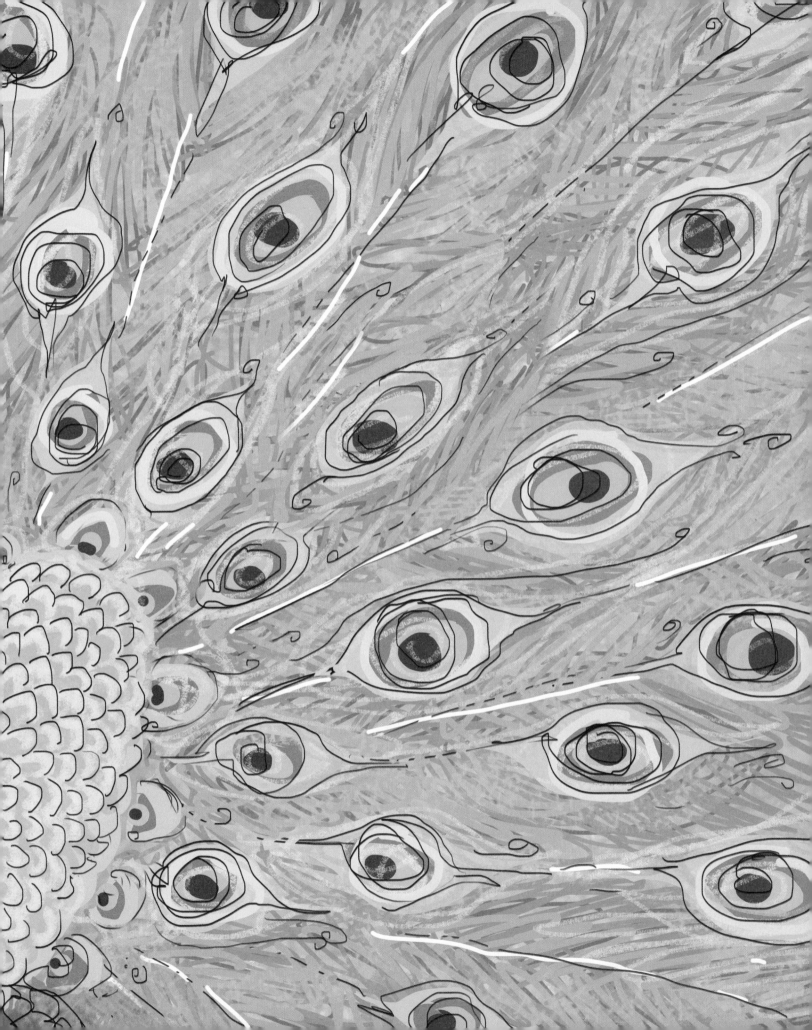

I spy with my little eye...

something with **grey** feathers
that sleeps when it's **light**
and flies when it's **dark**.

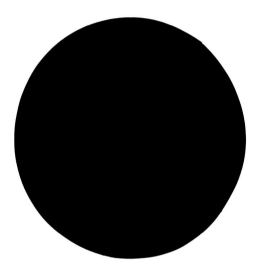

Twit-twoo!

I am an **owl**.

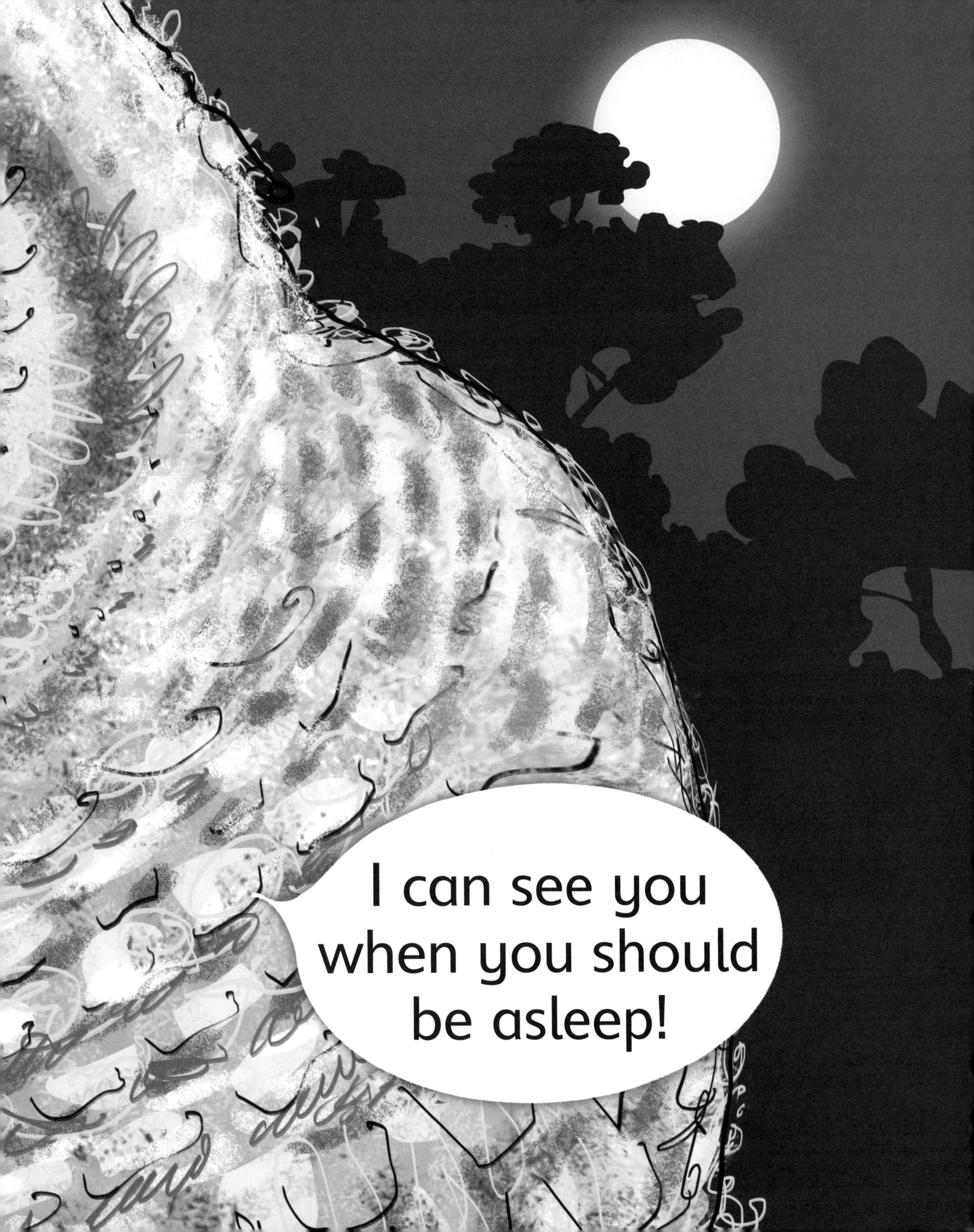
I can see you when you should be asleep!

What can you spy with your little eye?

To Felicity,
for keeping me aloft

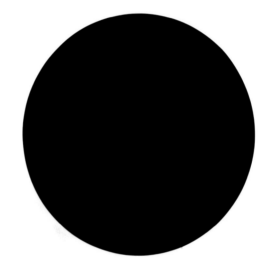

A BRUBAKER, FORD & FRIENDS BOOK,
an imprint of The Templar Company Limited

First published in the UK in 2014 by Templar Publishing,
Deepdene Lodge, Deepdene Avenue, Dorking, Surrey, RH5 4AT, UK
www.templarco.co.uk

ISBN 978-1-84877-884-9 (hardback)
ISBN 978-1-84877-989-1 (paperback)

Printed in China

For more information about Edward Gibbs and his books visit:
www.edward-gibbs.com